One Man's Journey
from
Heaven to Hell and Back

Peter Bering

One Man's Journey from Heaven to Hell and Back

Olympia Publishers
London

www.olympiapublishers.com
OLYMPIA PAPERBACK EDITION

Copyright © Peter Bering 2023

The right of Peter Bering to be identified as author of
this work has been asserted in accordance with sections 77 and 78 of the
Copyright, Designs and Patents Act 1988.

All Rights Reserved

No reproduction, copy or transmission of this publication
may be made without written permission.
No paragraph of this publication may be reproduced,
copied or transmitted save with the written permission of the publisher, or in
accordance with the provisions
of the Copyright Act 1956 (as amended).

Any person who commits any unauthorized act in relation to
this publication may be liable to criminal
prosecution and civil claims for damage.

A CIP catalogue record for this title is
available from the British Library.

ISBN: 978-1-80074-975-7

This is a work of creative nonfiction. The events are portrayed to the best of
the author's memory. While all the stories in this book are true, some names and
identifying details have been changed to protect the privacy of the people involved.

First Published in 2023

Olympia Publishers
Tallis House
2 Tallis Street
London
EC4Y 0AB

Printed in Great Britain

Dedication

To my mother Elizabeth Bering (Geml) and my grandmother Franciska Geml. Without their strength, love and support our family would not have survived and flourished.

Acknowledgements

Thank you to John Scannell for believing my story was worth telling. Thank you to my family for their support and their endless proof reading.

Author and Artist, Peter Bering

TABLE OF CONTENTS

Prologue: _____ 13
Chapter 1: My Heaven-Blessed Life _____ 15
Chapter 2: Heaven Fading: Prelude to a War _____ 23
Chapter 3: With War Comes the First Fires of Hell _____ 28
Chapter 4: The Beginning of the End: Hell's Insatiable Fury _____ 36
Chapter 5: A Concentration Camp in the Making _____ 40
Chapter 6: Life As it Became _____ 48
Chapter 7: The Will to Survive _____ 55
Chapter 8: Where There's a Will, There's a Way _____ 65
Chapter 9: Moving Towards Freedom _____ 72
Chapter 10: The Feeling of Freedom _____ 79
Epilogue _____ 87

Prologue:

What is the saying… Hate the sin, but love the sinner? In my life, I've had to learn how to forge that bridge, however tenuous it may have seemed at times, between my own suffering and the people responsible for it. It would have been easy to dismiss them as monsters, to see my captors as heartless villains single-mindedly intent on the destruction of humanity. To view them as cold-blooded killers whose life mission was tied to the phrase "mass atrocities". Indeed, what I saw and experienced transcends even the horrors of that phrase. In this context, I could let my hatred for the 'enemy' simmer until it consumed me. That would've been the easy thing to do—

Let me back up for a moment. I am a survivor. I prefer however to call myself a citizen, not of any one country per se, but of life in general. What does it mean to be a citizen? I frequently posed this question to my students, for I was also a teacher of art actually. Citizenship doesn't mean belonging to Canada, or Germany, or even to Serbia for that matter; rather, it means taking what society gives you, the good and the bad, and embracing it, using it to better yourself and broaden your mind. *Embrace the bad*, my students generally ask puzzled. Of course, perhaps more so than you would the good. If I've learned anything through the trials, the unspeakable terror I've endured, it is that you grow from your weakest, most vulnerable moments. You comprehend more keenly when you are at your lowest point. Because it is during such moments that you truly learn what you're made of.

It was in the life lessons, I've accumulated over the past eight decades and in my ability to find love in my heart even towards those who would see me tortured, that I came to understand what it meant to be a citizen of the world. I like the term well-visioned. I do my best to live up to this ideal. It's about stepping back and allowing yourself an all-encompassing view of the world and your consequent place in it, despite what may be immediately surrounding you. So, what have I discovered as far as where my place is in this world? I suppose it may be as a teacher, certainly as an artist. It is as, a devoted husband and father, a proud son for all those years. And I guess it is also as a survivor.

I went from a truly heaven-blessed life, into the very depths of hell itself and somehow, I came back again. I sought reprieve from the violence and death through the simple yet transformative beauty inherent in the world. I leaned upon what family I had left when the days were perennially overshadowed by the prolonged dark of one long unconscionable nightmare. And I dreamed of a time beyond the guns, the near starvation, the killings, the diseases and the camp.

I grew up in the former country of Yugoslavia in a village called Molidorf; well, that is its German name. In Serbian it is Molin and in Hungarian it is known as Molifafa. It no longer exists. The houses have long since disintegrated into nothing, businesses disappeared, the people unable or perhaps unwilling to forge ahead all left, and that's it. That's all it takes within the grand scheme of things to erase an entire village, a place that once embodied families, love, culture, education; like any other community it was comprised of so many wonderful, memorable parts. I suppose, given what happened there, the imprint of all of the good that was my hometown has been wiped out by the hell on earth it became. But I like to believe that the spirit of a once joyous Molidorf still guards its legacy.

I am not one to wallow in my pain or in those circumstances, however scarring, that can never be changed. I am not one to regret the life I've lived regardless of the context. In fact, on the contrary, I celebrate how I was able to persevere, all that I was able to build, the healing that my family, and I managed to undergo. Writing this has been perhaps one of the most difficult things I've ever done. Not simply in reliving the horrific memories I've long since attempted to block out, but in trying to pull from an entire life those crucial lessons learned. It was the playwright Henry Miller who once said: "In this age, which believes that there is a short cut to everything, the greatest lesson to be learned is that the most difficult way is, in the long run, the easiest." I suppose given what I went through, the most difficult was the easiest at least in terms of getting to this life now, and especially in terms of finding my way out of the fiery pits of hell into which my family and I were so brutally and abruptly thrust.

CHAPTER 1
My Heaven-Blessed Life

As I sit here, I am surrounded by art. I tend to see the world in pictures first. I suppose that's why I can trace the progression of my life through the images before me. Paintings of birds, fields and lakes literally flood me with that rush of youthful emotion that lifted my spirits as a boy, being hoisted up by my mother atop the dam and looking out over a vivid expanse of water that stretched almost beyond what the human eye could see. Even memories that weren't mine, I have worked to capture through painting.

Like this wolf, its eyes filled with the desperation of hunger, the primitive power of the animalistic… It is inspired by the story told to me about my great grandfather Anton Jakob. Wanting to expand his farm, he traveled to the nearby village of Toba to buy some piglets.

He left just as it was getting dark. With nothing but a boxed pole wagon, he traversed the pitted dirt road with only moonlight to guide him on his hour-long journey there and back. It was on his return that Anton encountered a pack of wolves—hungry wolves, emboldened by the strength of their own numbers. Unhitching the horses, he sent them running and then inverted his wagon so that he was now essentially caged in with the piglets completely surrounded by snarling wolves. He was confident the poles would hold. They did. When riderless horses returned home, his wife and family sent out a search party. Fortunately, he was found safe and sound still beneath that wagon with the piglets.

It is the vividness, the raw and intense emotion he must've been experiencing that spurred me to paint images I guessed he saw. It's always been that way with me. Art is as much feeling as it is color, shading, and dimensionality. Art is the expression of what feeling could be, the power it can have when you give your mind and heart up to canvas and brush. It doesn't have to be canvas and brush either—as I found out during those darkest days in hell; it could be something as crude as a finger on a grimy window, a stick on a dirty floor. Anything just to keep feeling. Anything at all.

I was born in 1938. Molidorf at the time was a village of 1200. It was a very low-lying region and was susceptible to repeated flooding, hence the dam that villagers regularly worked on. They sought to encircle the entire area with old potato sacks filled with clay. This method helped block the flood waters which threatened whenever the Danube and other smaller rivers overcame their banks. This also created several small lakes on the inside of the earthen walls.

My family was prosperous, especially given the relatively small size of Molidorf, to have two homes, 35 hectares of land, four horses and a threshing machine represented what was considered "well to do" at the time. It was in large part due to my grandfather, Wilhelm Bering, who'd been a soldier of fortune. He fought for Queen Victoria during the Boer War and was therefore able to purchase property upon his return. And once my parents, Jakob Bering and Elizabeth Geml married they inherited sizable parcels of land.

I don't know exactly what others thought of us, of our family that was for all intents and purposes rich, a family that had their fair share of servants regularly attending to their needs. But I know that my mother especially did her best to break down any barrier of pretension that may have existed based on financial status alone. At the end of everyday my mother would give the workers packages of food to take home to their families. In fact, she hired a Serbian carpenter to build her a number of chairs to sit around our personal table, as she observed: 'if we work together, we eat together.' She'd give away coats and extra clothes we had lying around the house when others didn't have the money to afford such things. Her heart in some ways knew no bounds; her spirit compelled her to do for others when they had difficulty providing for themselves.

I come from a family committed to treating everyone with dignity and kindness regardless of one's lot in life. My father was part owner of Long Lake (Lange Grundloch), purchased the first threshing machine in town, and was revered as a very capable but still fun-loving businessman—his prosperity was matched by his generosity toward those who worked for him. A good-hearted nature and what I would deem a quiet thoughtfulness seemed to go hand in hand for my family.

I look to my grandparents, my grandfather Joseph Geml in particular, and I consider how his studiousness intersected with his desire to help, and to heal. He became the village doctor specializing in herbal medicine; he was also, incidentally, Molidorf's newspaper editor at one time. But his life did not start out on the most auspicious of terms. He was born to a poor peasant family. With several brothers and sisters, none of whom could read or write, Joseph was resigned to the life of a field worker at a young age. And yet even that eventually became out of reach. One day, helping with the wheat harvest, the wind blew an awn into his eye. For those not familiar with wheat, an awn is the stiff bristle growing from the ear into the kernel. Unaware of the consequences, one of the peasants pulled this hastily from the boy's eye. The reverse barbs in turn managed to rip at the lens and essentially tear open the eye—he'd never see out of it again.

His parents, unsure of his future now that he was partially blind, sent him to a wealthy landowner to become a shepherd as it seemed he could see well enough for this job. And it is in the fields, watching over the flock, at the kindness of the landowner, that Joseph was given books and consequently taught himself to read. His parents were extremely pleased, not only because of his ability to read (and read to his siblings as well) but also because of the extensive vocabulary he soon developed. Joseph's mother and father started granting him a small portion of his wages which he saved and used to buy medical books.

Turns out, the young boy had a photographic memory. He easily absorbed the words and information before him courtesy of his cherished books. As a teenager, Joseph became known as the "young healer".

Of course, he lacked proper equipment and medications, so he came to rely upon the natural world around him, herbs, plants, that which he could concoct from the land itself. Joseph helped adults and children alike, devising cures for rashes, scabies, aches and pains. Consequently, it would be this ingenuity and his willingness to study and learn what he could about medicine that would be so vital to his family during the early days of the camp.

A doctor from the nearby city of Kikinda heard about the amazing boy healer and offered him a job as his assistant. He not only nurtured Joseph's raw talent but provided him room and board when needed; the doctor's wife becoming something of a second mother to him. And then in 1897, Joseph, who was nineteen at the time was sent to Belgrade for an Herbal Medicine course with a naturopathic doctor. He proceeded to become one of the youngest graduates with the highest marks—truly Molidorf's very own "wonderboy".

This is my heritage, the quietly strong, generous and resilient people who gave me my young life, my heaven-blessed young life. It's amazing now thinking back on the happiness, the beauty, the music that filled our days—the days before.

Genesis – Life Forces

I wrote a poem inspired by this painting; the imagery here embodies the quiet mystical strength of the simple beauty all around us, that from which we gain true insight. The poem reads:

Life Forces
Water on a blade of grass
Providing Life
Along its path
Man, in wisdom so does serve
All he sows
In his turf
On every level
In every state
To give is better than to take

My life forces, those of my family, were deeply entwined with an inherent need to give and to see people made happy—both before the devastation of the war and the camp and afterwards as well. I truly believe that this is what sustained us through the darkest days that we encountered. I learned from my grandparents and from my parents that genuine happiness is as much about looking outside of yourself into the hearts of others as it is about making sure your own heart was content.

My father in fact in those early days was known as something of a musician throughout Molidorf. His passion was to sing and spread joy, engender smiles with his music. He certainly did his part to try and bring happiness to those around him. Along with my uncle William (my mother's brother), they would frequently duet from the top of the church tower, they'd burst into impromptu song whenever the mood struck. Nightly they'd serenade the village—my uncle on violin or clarinet with my father singing. They even "toured" to neighboring villages, becoming known as the Molidorfer Band, and people seemed to love them. It was during one such concert that my uncle, playing at a wedding, met the town's postmaster who in turn introduced him to his daughter, Marija. In some ways it was love at first sight. She eventually became the postmaster for Molidorf and the two married. Their happily ever after was however to be tragically interrupted by the devastation of war.

I stop and reflect often on all of this… song, falling in love unexpectedly, men serenading an entire town from atop a tower. The romance and the inspiring hopefulness of it all. To go from that… to the other, is nearly unimaginable. And yet that was exactly what we did—we lived through the good and the bad, the heaven and the hell. Fortunately, even when my happy young life turned horrific, I still had people I loved and the memories of those no longer with me.

Dependable Poppies

    These poppies may have seen better days, been a little worse for wear, but they were there, strong, withstanding the elements, and what nature threw at them… There was still beauty in the utter resilience. I like to think of these as my family in some ways —whatever was thrown at us, enacted against us, we remained, the quiet strength of our resilience undeniable.

Family was and still is at the core of who I am. And despite the money we had once upon a time, the property we owned, those emblems of wealth that we were fortunate enough to have acquired, it was really all quite relative when it comes right down to it. A life is measured by how you live it, not by what you manage to accumulate during it. With each generation of my family, the people lived their life to the best of their ability—of this fact I am truly proud. Some had the trappings of good fortune, others not so much. There were phases during which we were veritable scions of a small Serbian town, and there were others where we lived in a home (if you could call it that) barely able to accommodate a single person much less four, the walls literally made of cardboard, as we huddled close together trying to recover from the atrocities that marked our post-war experiences, as we tried to erase the horrors that sadly you can never unseen.

CHAPTER 2

Heaven Fading: Prelude to a War

Shortly after the esteemed "wonder boy" of Molidorf, my grandfather, Joseph Geml, returned to his hometown to tend to the needs of the sick there, he was offered a job with a pharmaceutical company in Cleveland. Excited about the prospect and always an adventurous soul, he made the journey to America and lived there for eight years. Even after returning to Molidorf, he still received the Cleveland newspaper and diligently kept up with events abroad which is why the foreboding feeling, circa 1939… The Americans desperately feared the unequivocal rise of Hitler. It was evident in their tone, in their words, in the language condemning Germans for allowing this man to brandish and abuse such power.

My grandfather felt that fear radiating through papers that blasted headlines like: *Hitler Bombs Poland*, *Bomb: New Shock for Germans*, and *Hitler Plans New Ultimatum*. Frightened for his family, he strongly urged his two sons and sons-in-law to pack up and move to the US before it was too late. His eldest son, Peter, did in fact move his family to Windsor, Ontario. But the others did not heed grandfather's warning. My grandfather himself stayed in his beloved village of Molidorf. And consequently, Uncle Peter was the only man who came out of that war, out of the devastation alive.

Both my father and Uncle William were killed by the Russian army—years later we learned that Russian prisoners were conscripted to dig the trenches that would serve as rudimentary graves for my father and the rest of his regiment. I barely knew him. I certainly knew of him, I knew the love my mother held for him, the hope she clung to until the very end. I knew that when I was three years old, he went off to fight for the Germans. Stationed 20 km away in Kikinda he was able to come home on the occasional weekend. His arrival, never without the fanfare of song. In the middle of the night, he'd stand on the back porch and sing loudly, sweetly, calling out to his family, the woman he adored.

At first, he became a cook in the Yugoslav army and then segued into the same role with the Germans. My father's hands would never touch a gun; killing was not a part of who he was or what he could ever bring himself to do. This, a promise he made to my mother. In the end, he'd die in a hail of bullets raining down upon the men he was with, his friends. In war, the line between friend and enemy, between who you should trust and who is out to harm you can be blurry at best. But the one thing I take solace in, was that the men next to whom my father served were probably awed and entertained by his jovial nature, his incredible voice, the music that filled his soul and a smile that somehow, I am apt to think, made it seem like at least for a moment, things would be okay.

Where Eagles Fly

In some ways, I can envision my father as that eagle. Soaring to the tallest peaks, above the clouds even, looking down as his song and his spirit remain strong as ever. I know that despite the tragedy of his end, my father somehow managed to unleash the music within, making every precious second of his life here on earth something truly special.

In April 1941, without proper declaration of war the German army entered Yugoslavia from Romania, Bulgaria and Austria. The German troops conquered in a matter of days and Serbia was soundly occupied. This meant that all-ethnic German men were now re-drafted into the German army. And this, very much so, was that historical moment that changed not just the lives of those within Molidorf and Yugoslavia as a whole, but it would mark a dramatic shift in the way everyone came to see the world, at least in terms of what evil could do, the true strength and force of its uncontrolled power.

The phrase "death camps" immediately conjures images of horror, of terrors the likes of which many cannot even begin to wrap their minds around. Over six million Jewish people were killed in the most well-documented case of genocide in history. And that is solely the number of Jewish people. That does not include Soviet civilians, those with disabilities, those experimented upon, Polish civilians. The list is long. The unspeakable tragedy never to be forgotten.

There is also though a less documented instance of genocide associated with the second World War—that of which my family and I were a part. Hundreds of thousands of Germans would be moved to internment camps, later to be unveiled as death camps. Some historians have estimated that nearly one million Germans were consequently killed in these camps. The facts and figures are quite vague. But the reality of the atrocities enacted against Germans who weren't Nazis but rather civilians simply living their lives and trying to forge on in the midst of war is in many ways unbelievable. My father refused to kill other human beings regardless of what side they were on; my mother worked hard every day while her husband was gone just to feed her family and to help those who worked for her. My grandparents did their best to offer those within our village the benefit of their medicines and scientific knowledge so that there might be less suffering. We weren't monsters; we loved and cared for our fellow human beings, we only wanted to live peacefully. Germans apart from Germany. A family who'd forged out and built their lives in Yugoslavia—the last thoughts on their mind that they would be embroiled in a war for which they had no real context. No, we were far from monsters—we just happened to be German.

Sing Before It Rains

 You don't know when that storm is coming; you have no idea when the good is about to devolve into the bad, or worse, the unimaginable. Life, in many ways, is about song—the song of happiness, of hopefulness and love.

CHAPTER 3

With War Comes the First Fires of Hell

The next four years, from 1941 and 1944 would be some of the hardest we encountered; hardest, not most horrific, for that was to come *after*. We didn't live near the center of the war, we didn't know of all the atrocities being committed by Hitler and his army. We just knew that because we bore the blood of a German lineage, we were to follow the rules and abide by wartime standards. Such standards involved the women and elderly taking the reins in the village. As all of the men were gone, it thus fell upon those remaining to keep things going and maintain some semblance of "normal" for the children.

My mother, ever the hearty soul, was in some ways one of Molidorf's emergent leaders. She'd spent her life up until that point caring in one capacity or another for everyone from the poor gypsy woman to whom my mother gave our aging chickens so that the lady could feed a family of nine and not have to scrounge for the dead remnants of birds, to the laborers who worked for my mother wholeheartedly as they were in awe of her kind spirit, to the older people of the village who praised her resilience and admired her self-professed mantra that "hard work never hurt anyone".

In 1942, we experienced a serious flood in the midst of what was already an incredibly trying ordeal, given our location this was not uncommon. The crops were in danger; we fortunately had plenty of wheat and corn stored, but there were others who were not so lucky. My mother, along with her Serbian helpers, took our boat and where the waters had begun to recede went and planted crops in that portion of the field. During this time, given what was going on around us and within our very own village, my mom did what needed to be done, she extended her generosity to those who required it most.

She, in many ways, redefined femininity for me at this period of time. I look back now at those iconic images of Rosie the Riveter, a woman reborn as strong, independent, flexing her proverbial muscle such that had been previously hidden beneath a house dress and pearls, and in some ways, I see the grit of my own mother. Females weren't weak or scared, they didn't remain tucked away weeping for the war to end. The women like my mother understood that strength was at the heart of the feminine, as was determination along with the will to ensure that their families survived. The instinct for survival has an uncanny way of reinventing the perception of an entire gender.

Mother Earth

I quickly came to see during this period of my life why it is that the earth is thought of as a maternal entity in so many cultures and traditions. The 'Earth' is our most precious gift. All life comes from her and is attached to her. My own mother and Oma were the foundation of our survival back then. It wasn't even a choice really, it was instinctual for them, a part of their soul. They were light when otherwise it was dark, they were bounty when we had nothing, they were food when we should have been starving—they were my greatest blessing.

The Nazis conquered our town in 1939 and occupied our town until 1944. In 1940 they set up their headquarters in our town square. They were strict, especially regarding curfew. They were rowdy men that wined and dined, but were not destructive nor abusive. They set themselves up, not as guests, but as conquerors. My Oma just told me to be nice to the soldiers. They were the boss, but they did not tear down everything...that happened after they were driven out. During war, the line between friend and enemy is blurry, if not at times obliterated all together.

My grandmother once told me a story she'd heard from her sister who lived in a neighboring village. The Nazis, there were just as volatile and just as suspicious. There were two Jewish families who lived in the town, one owned a lumber yard and the other a bank. Those who'd run the bank had made it a practice to swoop in the minute someone couldn't make a payment, regardless of what they may have been going through, and take their land. Hard luck stories or tales of extreme difficulties fell on deaf ears with them—money was their master. Whereas the other Jewish family in town would help whenever possible. For those who did suffer hardship, they provided what they could, free of charge. And ultimately, when the Germans questioned the villagers regarding the presence of any Jews, the bankers were given up rather quickly while the others remained safely anonymous.

I know that war in and of itself is about death, loss, destruction, mayhem, the unimaginable. And yet, one of the things I learned perhaps more so than anything else during that period of time, what my family learned first-hand was that the human heart and human kindness do count—more than we realize. It truly is about how you treat others when not under a microscope, when not compelled to be nice for appearances sake, or propriety's sake, or anything like that, but because you believe in the power of goodness and authentically, you long to help.

Hollow and Hairy Woodpecker
   No action is too small
   For nature not to fathom
   Your foot that kicked a seed
   May start a growing action
   As the tall tree starts with one leaf
   Or a hollow with one scratch
   Tomorrow is a slow-built feat
   Made of actions from the past.

I was six years old; it was 1944, toward the end of October. By this point we'd come to a routine of some sort, albeit a tentative one, but we were learning to live life such as it was. The men gone, fear and uncertainty the pervading theme, yet we soldiered on in a manner of speaking. And then it all just suddenly changed. It was the middle of the night; loud and foreign sounds had become somewhat commonplace even during the darkest hours of the evening and yet this was far more invasive a noise than I'd heard before.

A tank, actually dozens of them, were passing by right outside our home, crushing up the cobblestone roadways as they moved. I'd never seen a tank before, much less an onslaught of this many chewing up and spitting out everything in their path. Perhaps this was the true face of war, I remember thinking to myself. A machinery of destruction that cares little for anything because when it comes right down to it, it has no feeling—just a jarring, brutal mass of metal embodying a force that will not be stopped. I guess though in some ways I read the scenario incorrectly. It was anger-fueled and unfeeling, yes, but it was a retreat. The Nazis, realizing their imminent defeat, had decided to pull up stakes in the middle of the night and leave Molidorf as hastily as they'd come in.

Last Light

In some ways, this painting reminds me of that night the Germans pulled out of Molidorf. We had no idea what lay ahead. We thought that we'd seen all the darkness there was; it was the light—our last for the time being—that they were taking with them and we in turn were about to become enveloped by perennial night.

History tells us about Hitler's many conquests leading up to and even during the war, his insatiable desire to grow the German empire, extend it throughout Europe and solidify this empire with the face of a master race. We see the distinctive images that are hard to unsee of the vast destruction that his ambition had upon the entire world, and of course on the Jewish population. As I think about it now, in the context of our 21st century world, I can't help but reflect upon that night of the German army's retreat from Molidorf. That was it—hell bent on conquering the world and recreating it into this distorted and monstrous Kafkaesque vision, they just stopped; they dropped it all and left. And the soldiers of the Third Reich for all intents and purposes, were on their way to once again becoming mere men, fathers, husbands and sons. I dare say that they weren't all monsters either, but many were unwilling souls caught up in one villain's evil dream, or rather nightmare. This is how I tend to look at the world and the people playing their parts in it. Letting evil win means seeing only evil wherever you look, even when staring directly into the hearts of those who, on the face of things, seem truly bad. It is far, far harder to see their humanity.

Chapter 4
The Beginning of the End: Hell's Insatiable Fury

While we were uncertain of the future, we knew better than to think that we were out of the woods and that a German retreat meant the return of our freedom, or our ability to enjoy life as we once knew it. In fact, if anything their departure foretold, just the opposite. With the Germans having left, Molidorf became a town occupied once again, this time however by the Russian army, who in tandem with Serb Partisans and a number of American advisors did not necessarily represent the winning side of war. When you are a village of ethnic Germans, I suppose there was no winning side of this war, regardless of how far from Germany you may have been.

We were considered Germans because we spoke the language and we did not resist the Nazis. However, we were Roman Catholic, pro-Western, Danube-Swabian farm people. We were surrounded by Serbian speaking, pro-Eastern, communistically inclined neighbours. They gathered every Danube Swabian village and hamlet and concentrated them into the towns of Gakova or Molidorf. Our pre-war village population was about 1,200 and grew into a concentration camp of 20,000-30,000 people of German heritage. This is why my grand-father Josef Geml told us that we were between a rock and a hard place and that we should move to America, but it was too late.

Survivor Buck

A buck's radar, his sense of sight, smell and hearing are always on high alert. In this painting I wanted to capture an aura of both vulnerability but also of his innate invincibility. It is his survival instinct as reflected even in the trees behind him and the moonlight as well, that allows him to remain aloof and camouflaged. We too would quickly have to figure out a way to remain under the guards' radar, virtually unseen.

Everything of value, from animals and furniture to machinery, was taken; either put on trains to be taken to Russia or brought to neighboring communistic towns.

The Russians, proved worse to contend with on a day-to-day basis. Women feared for their lives. Whenever they went out to get water from the nearby spring—we had no electricity or running water at this point—they'd "dress down". My mother herself succumbed to this charade as she was afraid of what the Russian soldiers might do. She'd even place a pillow under her shirt mimicking a hunchback. Attacks and consequent rapes on the women of the village were tragically not uncommon.

And it wasn't just the Russians. They'd chosen Serb Partisans to police the town. These were men who once upon a time had worked for the farmers of Molidorf, had even worked for my parents. Now, in light of how events turned out, the oppressed had literally become the oppressors. For those Swabian farmers who understood how to treat workers and viewed them as people rather than as laboring machines or worse, some sort of possession over which it was their job to tyrannically rule, the Serb Partisans left them alone. But for those who fell into the latter category, well, we heard stories of citizens being tortured or disappearing all together. My neighbor and his wife unfortunately never comprehended the value of simple kindness and subsequently treated those who used to work for them quite poorly. They were among the tortured.

Amber Moods

This may seem out of place here, but to me it captures the spirit of what every creature on this earth has the potential to be—what they need to be as dictated by the demands of common decency and kindness. This stalwart dog is many things, and my goal was to capture those diverse sides of her: she is submissive, assertive, guarded and loving, just as a human being has the capacity to be. You can protect yourself certainly and be on guard, but there has to be that part of you that embraces our commonality and finds the goodness within.

Then of course there were the Americans who set up camp temporarily in our village. They were there to ensure that peace reigned, and that law and order prevailed after the surrealness of war. I actually remember liking them. They were a bit more jovial and relaxed than the Russians. In fact, one of them even taught me some English words and phrases: "So long" and "Goodbye". He also eventually got me singing *Yankee Doodle Dandy*. My mom was not impressed, especially as one day he took it upon himself to go down into the cellar, lie under the wine barrel and open up the spigot pouring the contents directly into his mouth. He visited us almost daily, and when after about a week he stopped under our gate and called out "so long" and "be-good" I felt a little wistful; maybe I was just afraid to see him go. Or maybe, it was that niggling fear in my chest that the apparent calm, such as it was, was temporary at best.

CHAPTER 5

A Concentration Camp in the Making

There was a new government firmly entrenched in our town. It's funny, you reflect back to how things were, and it seems so distant, a completely separate time, populated by different people, people who woke up in the morning and went about their business collecting eggs and milk, getting the water, running and skipping and sometimes laughing while doing so. They were living a normal life, the life that every child should live, that every parent and grandparent should live. Sure, there were worries but they were of the mundane variety... so inconsequential really in light of the greater scheme of things—the scheme of things that has brought us to the realities of the camp.

I set here now in Canada reflecting and once again my worries are of the mundane kind. I worry about my kids for instance like any parent would, are they happy, do they have enough money, do they have someone to love. I do not have to worry about them being in danger of experiencing torture, or that they will fall ill because of deplorable conditions and never recover, or that one day walking through the field or down the street they will be shot and killed for no reason other than who they are by virtue of the happenstance of birth.

My mother, my grandparents had to worry about this. They didn't kiss us on the forehead and send us to school, lunch box happily clasped in hand as we trotted off to begin our day of education. They didn't see a beloved gaggle of children run out to the pastures to play, with a smiling 'just be careful' tossed after us. They would have loved to have been able to do that. They would have given anything for a "normal" day like that. It's so precarious really... What we think of normal, what *I* think of as normal now versus my normal then, such that was anything but.

Mother's Love

This moment is so simple. I wanted to capture not only the essence of the mother-child bond, but the sheer magic and beauty there is in such a basic occurrence: child sleeping tucked against its mother. I wanted to convey the utter peace and tranquillity of this scene. In those darkest days this kind of normal eluded us. I'm sure my mother would have given anything to embrace a moment such as this without the ever-present terror lurking within. I'm sure she would have wanted only the loving weight of her babies against her body as opposed to the impossible weight of the world.

It was April 1945; the Americans had all but gone. The Russians were now wholly in charge, with their Serbian enforcers ready and eager to keep everyone in line… Heaven forbid anyone should step out of line—and when I say that, when I say step out of line, I mean sneeze or hiccup without permission.

Everyone had their property confiscated. Class didn't exist, wealthy versus poor was no longer relevant; we were all relegated to slave status as the Russians took our homes, our wagons, our livestock, chickens, absolutely everything. Nothing remained as we were corralled as our animals had once been into homes designated as the living quarters for those being kept at the camp—and sometimes it wasn't even a house, some were kept in barns.

The animals were all gathered and taken to the train station. Perhaps a less harrowing detail given the fate of the people in Molidorf, they are after all just animals, but then again, I was seven years old and in some ways the animals were my best friends. My brother Bill and I had had a pet lamb, and as babies are wont to do, it grew into this majestic ram. Bengel, we'd named it, meaning little devil. We'd tie it to the wagon, and he would pull us around town, in the winter months, a sled, our own version of the Iditarod you might say. People would just laugh and wave watching the beautiful Bengel happily bleating with two boys in tow. Bengel was among the animals brought to the train station—even at the tender age of seven, I had no misconceptions about his intended fate. But he was a hard one to keep down. He jumped the fence of the holding area. And amazingly he found his way home. We were told that if we didn't bring him back, we would all pay the price. So, of course, we did. The cries coming from that ram as my brother and I walked away, leaving him to the slaughter that we knew though would not openly admit awaited, are still such that I can occasionally hear in the dark of my nightmares.

Where we lived then and under what conditions was a far cry from the life we once had—that elusive "normal" that was long gone. People were brought in from many neighbouring towns and provinces such as Banat. Generally speaking, there were anywhere from twenty-five to thirty people per "house" sometimes more; bedding was now that which had previously been reserved for barnyard animals—straw heaped in piles on the floor. Fleas and other such vermin were common as was, you could imagine, disease, not to mention starvation. We officially —or so history will tell us years later— became one of the largest concentration camps in Yugoslavia. Because of the war, the camp primarily consisted of women, children and the elderly— the men, most like my father and uncle, now dead. And so, those in charge began their cruelly systematic process of separating and relocating.

Women, those thirty-three years or younger, were sent to Russian labour camps. My aunt, Marianna Tensch my mom's sister, was among them—thankfully she would escape and join up a few years later. My mother lied about her own age, adding a few years. The thought of being separated from us was unbearable, and while the following year she'd be moved to a Russian outpost about ten km from town, we'd at least get to see her once a week—we did our best to live a lifetime in those few hours we were given. Children were thus placed into the care of older women, women otherwise unsuited to the hard labor of their younger counterparts. And the old men... most were shot; those allowed to live, did so in a separate area of the camp, though being "allowed to live" is a generous way of putting it. They were sent there until they starved to death—deemed unfit for a valuable commodity such as food.

My grandfather, the one-time 'wonderboy' of Molidorf dedicated to helping heal people, was one such older man. I visited him as often as I could possibly manage. And with each subsequent visit, I saw him grow thinner and weaker, until ultimately there was so little left, death was the only next step for him. He did what he could though. Blind by this point and near crippled from starvation, he still thought about those suffering throughout the camp. I would go there—I was living in a house with my grandmother (Oma) and about forty others (the number of people being brought into the camp grew daily in the beginning)—he'd feel my face, my arms and legs and ask if I was getting any food. He asked about the others, about my friends, my cousins. I described horrific images of distended bellies, swollen knees, and ankles, and skin covered in scabies. I described the way that so many walked about like zombies unable to reconcile one moment with the next. I described the nightmare that had become all our lives, even though my grandfather really didn't need a description...

Spirit of the Robin

This painting made me think keenly of our time in the camp. Robins in many cultures are considered divine birds, largely because their coming is a sign of renewal and rebirth. With all of the death and mayhem around me and my family, with all of the sickness and disease, I guess we just learned to look past it; you might say we looked for the spirit embodied by a small yet inspirational creature such as the robin. My grandfather, I know, even in his dying days, clung to the hope that we would at last realize that rebirth for which we dreamed every day.

Ever the healer, he would send my cousin Lisl and I to collect every weed we could find. Having somehow managed to finagle a couple of mostly mouse-eaten potato sacks, we scoured "our side" of the ditch grabbing every piece of plant life we could pull from the ground. After a successful scavenger hunt, we returned to our grandfather, bags of weeds accounted for. His lack of sight did not deter him; carefully feeling, smelling and even tasting every single weed, he'd put them into either good or bad piles. With the dozen or so "good" weeds we'd found, he instructed us to let them dry out in the sun for several days. He sent us on these weed finding missions as often as we could get out. Thinking back, it was an assortment of dandelion, rosemary and burning thistle among others. Beyond my scope, I just did as I was told, trusting in grandfather's knowledge and most importantly in his heart that wanted only to help those whom he loved before his own time ran out.

We'd hide the dried weeds in the attic and everyday Oma would crush some of them and put them into the pea soup. Bill and I had clear skin, no scabs. My cousin Lisl however was a different story… her head was covered in scaly patches, so much so that Oma had to cut out huge clumps of hair and consequently disinfect the area with the schnapps she'd kept hidden under her petticoat. Likewise, Lisl's skin was rife with scabs. Sure, enough she wasn't eating the soup infused with dried herbs—the taste was too bitter she'd complain. And then my grandmother all but forced it down her throat. Two weeks later both her skin and her head cleared up. My grandfather's laughter as I explained it to him was another sound that I will never forget from that period—a good sound, as few and far between as those were.

Sentinel Pine

I spent an afternoon with a centurion pine who held his ground for many decades. I thought of all the days, nights, seasons and storms that sand blasted every part of him repeatedly. But he stood steadfast, tenacious, tough and unyielding against fierce heat, cold, draughts and storms. Spread your branches with pride old centurion. I liken this pine to my grandfather. While in the camp, and even his life before, he weathered what most would run screaming from. His branches, time and time again, were my family's harbor. And for the moments we spent together, I am forever grateful.

One of the last memories I have of my grandfather was when visiting him, he thrust a small piece of corn bread at me. *Eat it,* he instructed. I looked at him, his gaunt frame, the hollowed-out eyes, the translucence of his skin, and I could not take it, despite how ravenously hungry I myself was. *Take it,* he insisted. I shook my head. But he would not accept no for an answer; he solemnly explained, *they are starving us anyway. Eat it,* he weakly smiled. Within a couple of weeks my Opa would be dead. His body tossed into a hole as big as a house with all the other bodies collected over however long a period before the mass grave was deemed filled. My brother, Bill, was one of the ones who dug the holes, and as horrific an experience as it must have been, one of the ones who collected the bodies in a two-wheeled hand cart—at least the boys given that particular job were kept well fed.

It only took a few months before the camp consisted only of women and children, the old men effectively killed one way or another. Our day-to-day became about survival. Food for instance… Thinking back on the "food," a word so innocuous and common, and yet it becomes the central component of your existence when it is scarce, or rather kept from you. Many of my memories from those years do indeed center around what food we did and didn't have. Pea soup, we were given, often garnished with black flies and other such insects. A couple of pieces of cornbread and that was it. Some of the Serbian guards to whom my mother had been so kind once upon a time had tried to sneak us food but that of course was dangerous. My brother, clever as he was—thinking creatively in some circumstances which often meant the difference between living and dying—made us slingshots from the rubber on our old billiards table before it was taken. These in many ways became our salvation. I became an ace shot—sparrows, pigeons, blackbirds, even the occasional crow.

The trick was how to clean and cook the birds without anyone seeing. Oma still had a small cast iron stove. We dug up corn cobs from the pig manure for burning which made for a pretty decent fire. In a large kettle she'd boil her blankets and sheets in order to cook the fleas out of them. Meanwhile, after having cleaned the day's catch in the outhouse, she'd sneak them into the kettle beneath the laundering linens. No one was the wiser. There were so many people starving, people, children dying weekly as a result of the lack of food. Our meager catch really only fed us, and barely even that, if you consider how small these types of birds truly were. I know my grandmother's heart broke not to be able to share with the others in the house—but there wasn't enough, there simply wasn't enough.

Do generosity and magnanimity of spirit just go by the wayside when faced with these types of circumstances… Is it easy to watch someone else suffer so that you can live? I realize now that's not it at all. Self-preservation, this urge to survive, is instinctual. If we'd shared those tiny birds, divided them up among dozens it would have been to a futile end. Our situation, our position made it so that nothing we could have done would have mattered, not really. There is moral responsibility and yet when there is certain death staring you in the face, you understand this responsibility differently—it comes to encompass a different set of beliefs and urgencies. For my grandmother, she understood that the children she loved were withering away unless she did something about it. This, in fact, was something she could do. She could not save an entire camp, the entire village of people, but she could at least try to save us.

CHAPTER 6

Life As it Became

Beyond the lack of food, there was rampant disease. And with no medical care of which to speak, sickness became one of the leading causes of death among those in the Molidorf camp. You can't possibly imagine what it's like to watch your friends, your neighbors, people you love die because of something that was otherwise so very treatable. But given the conditions, the pure squalor in which we lived, even medicine, in some cases probably wouldn't have helped.

In 1946 I came down with malaria. My family huddled around me fearing the worst. My mother decided that with my brother she would try and sneak to some Hungarian friends she had in Toba and get whatever medicines they could. Their journey did not go well…

Escape is not something you think of in reality, but rather in the abstract, when you are in a situation like we were. The word itself so ungraspable and yet it is the only thing you dream of, at times the only thing you can focus on. There were a couple of occasions that year during which one or more of us tried to escape. I was a child, I was going along and doing as I was told, but I'm not sure that I honestly ever pictured something other than the grim reality in which we were ensconced. I don't think I ever got my head truly around the idea of "escape", around something other than life as it had become.

Genesis – Emetic Russula

In the most trying moments, those times when we thought death inevitable, even when we were unable to see beyond the heartbreak of a failed escape, or a beating, or some other form of torture, I believe that there were still seeds deep down inside of us, just waiting for a hint of sunlight in order to grow. And in large part that's what this painting expresses—even amid the trash of the forest floor, there is something waiting to be touched and nurtured back to life again.

As I mentioned, my mother and Bill had attempted to make their way into Toba to get me the medication I needed, or for that matter, whatever medication they could get their hands on. It was more than just them going through—there were a number of people heading toward this elusive destination known as "escape". It didn't take long before the group was discovered. Shots were fired, people were hit, many died, many were wounded—thankfully my brother and mother were among the wounded, as they were badly beaten and tossed into the wet basement. Bleeding and shivering throughout the night, they too became gravely ill. The next morning brought even more horrors. In order to set a clear precedent, the Partisan guards singled out several of the wounded and shot them on sight—a lesson to deter any future escape plans anyone might be harboring.

My mother has never been a deeply spiritual woman. But this was one of those moments in which she felt God's presence lifting her up, carrying her through the horrors of this particular trial. One of the guards had previously worked for us. She could only assume that her kindness and generosity, such that she had once been in a position to convey, is what saved her and Bill's life in that instant. The guard recognized her, he also recognized that they were terribly sick and in a bellowing voice, exclaimed: "What kind of disease are you trying to pass on to us?" At which point he then beckoned for a Serbian woman to come take them away—also someone who used to work for my mother. With tears in her eyes, the woman instructed them to go home.

There was another instance… this time we all went. My mother had made contact with an American who'd stayed behind. He wanted to help as many Swabians as he could to escape. And in some cases, he was successful. My mother, filled with stories of how he'd enabled many to get to the freedom they so desired, paid him with jewelry she'd hidden in manure piles. In the middle of the night, we silently crept away from the town that was once our home, and had become our nightmare. I knew there was a tangible nervousness, fear, excitement too in a strange sort of way. I understood that we were leaving the only thing we knew for that about which we had no idea really. And when I heard the gunshots, I knew that escape, such as it was, wasn't to be.

Not only were guns fired, but Partisan guards were clubbing people in the heads with the butts of their weapons. They were punching and kicking, people strewn about lying bleeding and wounded, some dead. The younger, more able-bodied women were separated out—meaning my mother among others—and the rest of us, those still alive were herded back home, again, such as it was.

Home—this new incarnation of home—was a far cry from what I'd ever known and yet there was a connection to it. It'd become part of this life, and as unspeakably horrific as this home was, it still embodied a part of me, my family. Such an arbitrary term, home, and such a necessary one too. I sometimes think that perhaps holding onto that ideal of what a home truly symbolized is what in part helped get me through it all. I'm not sure, but when you have nothing and your humanity is all but stripped away, you find comfort in the unexpected, even if it isn't intended to be of any comfort. It's amazing where the mind and heart are capable of finding value sometimes.

We were frantic about my mother's fate. In the dark, we had no clue as to even what direction these women had gone. I think my grandmother and possibly my brother assumed the worst—we had no other blueprint. We had a map that pointed to torture, starvation, disease; we had a map that ultimately led us and everyone we loved to death. And so, when a couple of hours later my mother walked through the door, we were beyond shocked. At first, I think the shock of it all was so intense that we barely noticed the fact that her clothes were soaked in blood; she quickly allayed our fears and reassured us that she was not hurt—turns out, it wasn't her blood.

She told us the story of what happened that night. In some ways, I can see it playing out in my mind even though I wasn't there. Perhaps it is because of the vividness of her details, the shaky somberness of my mother's voice and the way that she seemed almost disembodied as she spoke, like she'd temporarily left her soul and spirit behind because otherwise, she wouldn't have been able to cope with the fallout, and still maintain her sanity at any rate.

The women were taken and then lined up. It was quite easy to see the guards' intent—they were going to execute the women who'd tried to lead their children and elderly parents out of the camp. And yet again, the hand of God coupled with the big-heartedness of my mother in her life 'before,' saved her from certain death. Three of the Serbian patrolmen had previously worked for us. My mother recognized them at once. One approached her in order to blindfold her; as he was applying the blindfold, he whispered in Serbian (which incidentally my mother spoke perfectly) "when you hear the bang, drop your head and pretend you're dead". That, she explained, was the easy part. It was when her body was hoisted onto a wagon full of corpses, warm blood drenching her, soaking into her clothing, the sanguine smell of life eking away, dripping out of these women, women she knew—that was the part she will never ever forget, she said. The guard had told her to roll off the wagon once they hit the cemetery road, make it look like her body fell off after hitting a bump. And here she stood… miraculously, but also because of who she'd been, the courtesy and humanity she'd extended to all of those who worked for her. In her kindness, you could say, there was life.

Hell, and Heaven on Earth

  Make no mistake about it, there is both here on this planet, during our brief stay. We get to experience the joy and the love that comes from the people in our lives. We unfortunately also get to experience evil—sometimes in its most malicious forms. This particular ordeal that my mother endured was the epitome of what evil is capable of, and yet buoyed by her heart and her generosity of spirit, you could certainly say that heaven played a role here too.

In some ways, I relive this horror through my mother's recollections. Actually, in many ways I do. Because she was an adult and a healthy woman in the camp, she was exposed to so much of the torture, the brutality, the gruesomeness that had come to subsume life in Molidorf. I suppose that was a misnomer though—this wasn't Molidorf; this did not at all resemble the place I knew. This was a concentration camp. At the time, we knew little about what had happened to the Jewish people. Immediately after the war, we were dragged into this reality and so we'd been cut off from what was happening within the world. All we understood was the immediate present: the camp in which we were prisoners, slaves, targets, objects of scorn. We weren't even really seen as human anymore.

My mom recounted a time she was part of a forced march—enslaved women carrying bundles of wood for many kilometers. The Serbian guards would stop repeatedly and whip and beat those who lagged behind or those, their strength waning, who dropped pieces of wood. My mother tried to help. Listening to the cries of pain and agony was too much for her to bear. And yet, she too was whipped; until that is, one of the guards, again a former worker, stepped in. He explained that my mother was an excellent cook and thus would be an asset at the Stalash (Russian outpost). From then on, while her life was still excruciatingly difficult, she at least got food and was able to bring us every Sunday.

CHAPTER 7

The Will to Survive

With my mother being relocated to the Stalash, I was understandably terrified. In this world, this new reality with which we were faced, it wasn't as much about the horrors that you daily confronted—the disease, the beatings, the torture, but rather, perhaps the scariest part was what you didn't see. The night my mother had escaped just shy of being executed, it was the not knowing that allowed my imagination to run amok. When waking up in the morning and your foremost thought is simply surviving the day, your mind tends to venture into dark and emotionally debilitating places. With her gone, I conjured scenarios that no small child should ever have the capacity to conjure. I prayed, I cried, I waited. And in the waiting is sometimes when the darkness comes.

Swamp Transformation

    As I said, during this particular period, when my mother was taken to the Stalash, life shifted dramatically—yet again. In Swamp Transformation, I try and depict how one small hiccup, one slight adjustment to an ecosystem can completely change the look, the feel and the spirit of something even as seemingly inconsequential as a swamp. From life to death and back again…

Fortunately, my mother was a fighter, always has been. She knew how and when to put her head down and work, but perhaps most crucially, her kind spirit (both past and present) is what got her through the toughest moments. At the Stalash she tended to the animals, milked the cows, cleaned the stalls and cooked for the Partisan guards. They liked her cooking, turns out they liked her too. Which is why they let her eat all she wanted; they even gave her leftovers—most importantly, they let her come back to us every Sunday.

    We'd wait at the very edge of the village, or rather, the camp. I looked out across the fields and in that far away image of my mother making her way towards us, I felt this indescribable modicum of hope. When you're a kid, your mother is that symbol of home—she is the warmth you've always known, the tender smile that makes the bad go away, the twinkling eyes that promise tomorrow will be better. And as she came towards us those Sunday afternoons, bag of food in hand, I felt all of these things rush over me. Despite how I looked, how thin I was, how starved I was for a life that wasn't filled with more of the same desperation and horror, that image of my mother gradually coming into focus from miles away was the promise that somehow this would ultimately be okay. Somehow, we'd make it out alive and back to a life of family, of smiles and celebrations, of music and laughter. It may have been naïve of me—after all I was only eight years old at the time—but this weekly return of my mother was tangible. I could hug her and smell her familiar smell and hear the voice that had been music to me since birth. And I guess I knew in the end, one way or another, she'd make it okay. Her leaving Sunday nights was terrible, soul crushing in some ways. But then, I would have the following week again—the brief gift of my mom returned to me, still alive and still determined to see us all through this.

Beyond these fleeting yet full moments with her, there was something else to which I clung desperately in an attempt to circumvent the life I now lived and escape to the life I would hopefully one day realize; there was art.

Opus

I was watching Andrea Bocelli and Celine Dion sing to a spellbound audience of thousands in Central Park in New York City. It was dark, cold and nasty out, yet the audience wanted more. You could tell, they were cheering and clamoring. Those beautiful clear voices reverberated into the night and kept the audience warm. In thinking about this painting, I kept hearing in my head: "The warmth and clarity echoing into the night." Art can do that; it can transcend the bounds of cold and dark. It can bring warmth and light to the most despondent. It can save your spirit when you aren't even sure you have a spirit left to save.

In the most heinous of tragedies, one has no choice but to draw upon their own will to live, otherwise you don't stand a chance. Once you give up, once you tell yourself there is nothing waiting beyond… this, your only fate is to be subsumed by the bleakness around you, and you inevitably start down that path toward hopelessness. But this wasn't me, not yet. I had hope still. I had that Sunday visit, her reassuring maternal embraces, and I had my escape into the world of beauty and art.

I don't consider myself particularly strong or resilient or courageous. I do consider myself a survivor. And one of the main reasons I was able to survive was because I refused to see only the destruction reflected back in the mirror into which they were trying to force us to look. Life was more than this. It had to be.

Life was the birds still flying free above the village I so once loved. Life was the flower that even though trampled by warring boots managed to bloom again. Life was even the wheat in the fields that in its final phase of life still clung to this effervescent golden color. I could see that—I could never not see it, regardless of how much they hurt us and tried to break our spirits.

There was a vineyard just on the other side of the berm, a barrier we were not allowed to cross. Two of my best friends (twin boys) had done so, tempted by the delicious looking grapes that hung on the vines ever so close. When you're hungry, truly hungry, food is more than just daily sustenance, it is a reason for, in some cases, everything that you do. And there are moments when looking at something as simple as a cluster of grapes that the reason provided by the food outweighs the dangers you otherwise dismiss.

They were running back, arms loaded with all the grapes they could pluck in a hurried few minutes. I was waiting for them, drawn to the promise of what they carried and also to their smiles. A guard spotted them and began shooting. Do you know what a gun blast sounds like up close? Not up close as in standing beside someone at the firing range and casually watching as they take target practice, but as in, those bullets are aimed at you, and you are an eight-year-old child and you have no true concept of death other than what you've been hastily introduced to. You still though, don't honestly think it's going to happen to you. It can't, right? You're only a child.

Both boys were killed instantly. Those boys, my dear friends had curly blond hair and blue eyes. They had decades of life to go. They wanted grapes, that's all. They wanted to remember what life felt like once upon a time. Even though I was so young, their faces have never left me. In some ways, I have never not seen them running out of that forbidden vineyard, bearing those grapes.

Luna Moths

    These moths live for but a week. Their stunning green wings spread out about five inches. As caterpillars they hungrily devour the leaves of the birch trees and then blossom into almost surreal and ethereal like creatures just to perish so soon. I can't help but think of those boys, and what kind of wonderful human beings they could have grown into.

I did not escape unharmed, but I did escape with my life—which was everything. By the time I got home my shoe was filled with blood. I'd been shot in the left leg. Oma set to work at once. Something about this camp, this time, had changed us all and for her it became about immediacy. Emotions had to be kept in check as taking care of the emergencies associated with the here and now left no time for wallowing or even crying really.

She disinfected her jack-knife with her bottle of schnapps—that bottle got a lot of use and amazingly seemed to be some sort of magically eternal wellspring for her. She then jammed her handkerchief in my mouth as she set to digging out the bullet. Thank God in some ways I don't remember that exact pain. I was told, I passed out three times during the process. After all was said and done, she poured schnapps down onto the raw wound by way of disinfecting it. The burning was beyond excruciating—that part I do remember. It was to teach me a lesson; except the types of lessons you learned here weren't your typical childhood lessons. The takeaway was pure survival. She tied a clean blouse around it as we of course had no bandages and then she bade me go clean out my bloody shoe. Afterward, Oma informed me that it wasn't a bullet she'd dug out of my leg. The guard was again one who knew us, knew my family, had eaten at my parent's table and so he'd shot at the ground to scare me. A stone had then ricocheted into the flesh of my thigh.

It was this wounded leg that brought me to the escape that was art. The leg was terribly swollen and the accompanying pain nearly unbearable at times which meant there was a great deal of sitting around for me. I couldn't run or even walk, certainly couldn't climb trees. My brother Bill had fashioned a crude looking crutch but that only helped so much. So, I would find myself sitting on the porch quite often. And as I was a small boy, boredom inevitably gave rise to fidgetiness which found me using sticks lying within reach to draw pictures in the sand. Birds, rabbits, trees, farm animals…Whatever I saw or whatever I could conjure from memory I drew. Kids who were nearby, haggard looking kids, the life all but sucked out of them would still manage a smile when looking down at what I'd done. You see it wasn't merely a way for me to momentarily revert to a life I once knew, it was a respite for them too.

They'd ask me what the images were (those they couldn't tell upon first glance). We'd make a game of it sometimes. The tragedy that had resulted in my temporarily out-of-commission leg had actually brought me that which would come to define the rest of my life: seeking life's peace, its beauty and its treasures as buried as they may be at any given moment, through artistic expression. Regardless of how young I was and the circumstances surrounding that youth, I still inherently knew that this is who I was supposed to be. I could create these vignettes of hope and beauty and at the very least make those with usually heavy hearts smile for a moment.

The irony of making something beautiful out of dirt was lost on me then. Now, however, I see how symbolic that life moment truly was. This camp in which we were imprisoned was that dirt. Most times, I didn't think things could get any worse or we could get any lower and then lo and behold young boys get killed on the spot, or a group of women are murdered execution style, or old men are subsequently starved into their graves. But here, here was purpose beyond the senselessness of our collective deaths. And here was one boy's ability to transcend, because his spirit, for whatever reason, remained strong.

Storm Wave

A residual effect of the devastating Hurricane Sandy that brought destruction to so many on the east coast… I watched the waves roil, become angrier and angrier. I thought it important at the time to take this image of something so darkly ominous and turn it into a painting that could be both beautiful and foreboding too. And that was what I strived to do interned in that camp—find the dark and make it something that mattered to me and to those who looked at my drawings…in a different way, a special way.

My canvas selections grew to include the mud out by the well. The well became this quaint gathering place where we'd talk almost like normal; it was amazing in some ways. People dared to talk about a life "after" whenever they congregated around that well, they dared to dream. There was this one boy who slept by the side door nearest the well. Whenever I went out there, he'd smooth out a patch of mud and ask me to draw in it.

I remember his gaunt and starving face. I also remember how he smiled whenever I'd completed one of my mud masterpieces. It was perhaps the greatest accolade I've ever received to date.

In our house the heat generated by all those bodies crammed within, not to mention the warmth from the old wood stove, would cause the single pane window to steam up—I took my finger and drew in that as well. The act of drawing itself ultimately became need for me, much as food, water and shelter. And it wasn't solely for my own escape or pleasure, but because I knew I could add something of value and of worth to the desolate conditions which otherwise offered nothing but more blackness.

CHAPTER 8

Where There's a Will, There's a Way

In the latter half of 1947, there were shakeups at the camp. I know it's hard to imagine that it could get worse, that more of the "unknown" could be just on the horizon. And yet, that's exactly what we were facing after nearly two years of our grim post-war reality. Most of the people in Molidorf were being relocated to what we later discovered was the town of Gakowa. At the time, we had no clue as to what was going on or where we were being taken. For all we knew, rounded up late at night and brought to the train station, we were off to certain death. As I said, the unknown is many times far, far worse.

My mother meanwhile was still laboring heavily at the Stalash. She'd heard of the relocations and begged to be able to go with us. This time however, they would not relent. Instead, the commander offered to have her taken to the train station so that she could say goodbye and bring us some food. My mother's life, her mission at this point in time was to keep us alive by whatever means necessary. It didn't matter how hard she had to work or what she had to do, as long as her family survived. Imagine, if you can, being separated from your children and mother; not to mention everybody else so cruelly taken. And then being told they were to be transported somewhere unknown. For all you were aware, there was a mass grave waiting at the other end of that train ride. Remember, my mother had seen these mass graves firsthand; my brother had been among the ones assigned to dig them.

They did take her to the train station the night we left. Except, she was too late—our train had already departed. We never got to see her—she never saw us. And so, for our family, the next few weeks, regardless of where we tried to direct our minds to go, it became a matter of thinking the absolute worst.

Waiting Egret

In preparing to paint this image, I remember watching this bird wait daily. For the minnows to come in, for the timing to be perfect. It didn't really look all that concerned that things just wouldn't work out as he wanted them to—he just intuited they would. Yes, we often thought the worst, but honestly something in me held together and let me know, whether by some sort of divine intervention or the power of love, that if I just waited, it would work out as it was supposed to.

When we got to Gakowa, our "new" concentration camp, there was very little difference. It was simply getting used to this normal as opposed to the one we'd just left. In both cases, it was still a prison. Now, we had no idea where my mother was, if she was even alive. It was weeks of not knowing. Those weeks perhaps the slowest we'd endured thus far. Every time a wagon came by, my heart leapt into my throat with the thought that his could be her, finally! She would miraculously be brought back to us by the grace of God and the feel of her arms around me was so real in my imagination that I sometimes wept with pure joy. But then the wagon would keep on driving, right by where we bunked. And my mother was not among the passengers and her smell so relevant in my nostrils, her embrace so keen in my memory, started to get further and further away. Soon, I was afraid I wouldn't remember at all anymore.

While we were acclimating to our circumstances, my mother it turns out had fallen ill, gravely so. So sick in fact she could no longer work. Perhaps it was her broken heart that hastened the illness. They say that stress kills, that extreme sadness weakens. In this case, my mother, out of her mind with her worries and fears of what'd become of her family, probably made her body far too vulnerable. There were Serbian women with whom she worked that took pity on her and went to the commanding officer, pleading for her release. They explained that given her state she might not make it, much less ever be able to work again in the Stalash. There was a wagon going from Molidorf to Gakowa, transporting the sick people. All my mother was to them was a waste now, the women tried desperately to reason. It worked. She was released from her duties.

This time, after weeks of being immersed inside of our own worst fears, this time the wagon did indeed carry my mother. It brought her back to us! It was a reunion—not under the best of circumstances of course—but maybe that's what made the meaning of it so much more profound. We were imprisoned, we were sentenced to this life in which the whims of tyrannical guards essentially dictated whether we lived or died, but by some miracle, we'd found our way back to each other. And that was truly a blessing.

Shortly after her convalescence my mother was put to work making bricks. They could see that she was strong and healthy; they were not about to let a potential worker go. Loading the brick kiln, she was tasked with making upwards of a thousand bricks per day. It was back breaking work in the most fundamental sense and yet my mother did it happily. She was with us after all. In fact, she grew accustomed to the heat of the furnace, preferring it to being out in the cold. She was diligent about her business and the guards took notice. They commended her for her work ethic. She was even, on occasion, given food to bring home to us. Not to mention a nearby Hungarian farmer who would sometimes give her beets and potatoes which my mother would roast in the ovens and then bring back to feed her family. Simple things meant a great deal. Just as my drawings in sand and mud had come to emblematize a different world, a world that I could tolerate, these potatoes kindly given to my mother were also symbols: of the inherent good that still did exist within the human heart, though it may have been obscured in our eyes. It was a symbol of the fact that we did still have one another, and we could sit down and eat together—roasted potatoes a veritable feast.

And we certainly made the most of it. When not at the kiln, my mother would miraculously scrounge pencils and some paper and give us our daily reading and math lessons. She insisted that if we let them take everything, to include our willingness and ability to learn, then we truly would be defeated. Hard work was not only done with your hands, according to my mother, but with your minds as well. She also stayed in touch with the women living in camp houses close to ours. She'd hear stories of younger people being taken away to God only knows where. And her fears, with every story she heard, were always reignited.

Reawakening

    Reawakenings generally have a positive connotation. Along the same lines as a revelation or a

    rebirth... But they are not always easy, and sometimes can be about navigating difficult terrain, even treacherous terrain. In this new phase of camp life, there was a bit more hope certainly and that proverbial light perhaps at the end of an otherwise endlessly sinister tunnel, but then again there was still much danger, enemies lurking, upheaval still rampant.

For my mother, while she may have endured the tiresome work and following orders, she still wanted more for her children especially. I honestly think she'd rather give her own life than have to watch us grow up as prisoners always terrified of the unknown that each new day could conceivably bring. This wasn't the childhood she'd ever planned for us—then again, this wasn't a life that anyone plans.

    Now that we were in Gakowa we were closer to the Austrian border. The potential for freedom was there, though still an incredibly dangerous risk. To save us all, my mother was willing to take that risk.

She'd located someone who was organizing to take a group of thirty over the border late at night. We gathered in the barn on the edge of town. The nervousness, fear, excitement, hope, desperation, all of it was palpable that evening. I don't necessarily remember every detail, but I do remember that heaviness and suffocation of feeling in the air. All of us, the emotion right there on our sleeves. You become used to steeling yourself against any such emotion because when you're in a place like the one we were in, it is dangerous to feel. But not that night. Or any of the nights during which the faintest hope of escape was possible.

Just as we'd taken off toward that elusive border, a young child began to cry, and that was all it took.

Shots were fired, into the air thank God. Yet, while no one was killed, the younger women among the group were rounded up and taken to a room in which they were locked in. My mother was one of them. And yet this time, she would not be kept from her family. She explained to us later that she managed to finagle a window open and climb out; despite the fact that the other women begged her not to as she would surely get shot upon being discovered, she persisted. She needed to know that we were safe, and she would not be separated from us for another minute longer than she had to be.

Devotion

I will always firmly believe that the strongest glue holding the people of this world together is that of familial bonds, in particularly that between a parent and child, what's more a mother and child. A mother will risk anything, she will never stop watching over those children, even if she has to bring harm unto herself to do it.

CHAPTER 9

Moving Towards Freedom

My mother is an amazing woman; my grandmother is an amazing woman. I'm sure I've said that, but it stands restating. Our family is at the heart of why we came through the horror of it all. And the strength of that family, at that time, rested deep in the souls and spirits of its matriarchs. After the first attempt to flee Gakowa, my mother resolved that we would try again. She would get us out of there; she would show us how life was meant to be lived even if it required her to die trying.

This time we crept away from camp in the middle of night just below the windows of the guard house—their guns always at the ready. Taking further precautions, the mouths of the younger children were stuffed with handkerchiefs so as not to have a replay of what had occurred during the last attempt. Essentially, it was a series of fields that lay between our group and freedom. We knew what getting to the other side stood for, and so through the pain and aching muscles and tired bones, through the diarrhea and dehydration, we kept on going. Imagine racing toward that finish line, except you're not in it for a medal or trophy, you're in it for your very life, for ultimate survival, and to find the happiness and peace that has eluded you for years. We were those marathon runners but on this particular leg of the race, absolutely everything was at stake.

After about a week, we finally crossed the Hungarian border—this however was not the final destination. We were warned actually that some Hungarians were quick to call the guards on those who sought refuge on their side of the border. We came to a small church; thankfully the priest spoke German. He directed our group toward a safe place. His kindness and warmth were something which seemed strange, I remember thinking. For so long we'd been eyed as prisoners, treated no better than animals on most days. Yes, there was the occasional mercy shown us usually by those who'd worked for my parents "before". But then as the years in the camp deepened, as the torture intensified, we felt more and more isolated from the inherent warmth and joy that is supposed to exist in the world. Our world was cold, our world was about death. The stares became icier, the barks angrier, the pain and destruction more widespread. But here, these kind people were helping us.

The priest directed us to a small potato farm. The woman who lived there spoke a little German; my mother meanwhile did her best to convey what she needed to in Hungarian. Language barrier aside, they became fast friends. And for once in a long while, we had something we'd all but given up on, hope.

Updraft
 It's a truly amazing thing to look out over the world from this perspective and think: it is waiting for me, I am actually a part of the landscape, of nature, of the beauty I see before me. I am not a prisoner and I am not a slave—I am like the birds; whose flight takes them where their hearts lead. This was our moment of hope—finally.

They paid us to dig potatoes and pick grapes. They gave us shelter and beds with real mattresses! It was hard work, but it was our work. We received compensation for it. We weren't forced into labor but appreciated for our efforts and energy. And in the two weeks we stayed, a bond formed between us all. When it was time to go (we couldn't afford to remain in Hungary for too long), we were of course sad to leave this family that had taken a risk in giving us safe harbor. They would become those among many from here who would touch our lives simply through their kindness and generosity of spirit.

The next stop was the Danube. To get out of Hungary and into Austria we had to cross the enormous river. I remember it was a rickety old bus that took us to the barge. It would not be the first vehicle of this journey that seemed a rather precarious way to travel. But freedom was risk; freedom was also having faith… a lot of faith.

After crossing, we came to a farmhouse. By this point we'd been en route for three weeks. The journey was taking its toll on my mother and especially on Oma. They were drained; they did not give up, but you could clearly see the mental and physical exhaustion consuming them. Here is where I think more so than all of the horrors my mom had endured, more than being carted with dead bodies, than watching Russian soldiers drive their bicycles over the top of the fallen, than being beaten and threatened, here is where the resilience of my mother came shining through. When you are immersed in a situation that in some ways eludes even description, there's something that goes on autopilot inside of you. You can't cope with events and atrocities the likes of which we faced without somewhere, some place in your mind going into moments of shock. The involuntary thus takes over and you move and speak and act but you do so outside of yourself almost, if that makes any sense. Without question, my mother's heart and strength carried her through, but in some instances, it was also her ability to just keep going and block out what would have otherwise shaken her mind and soul to their very core. But here, during this, our escape, she came back into herself. Weariness would not defeat her—her perseverance was too strong for that.

The farmer offered to take us in his Model T truck to the final crossing: The River Ruba. This truck had no sides. You could barely call it a vehicle. We held on for dear life as he whipped through pastures and fields under cover of darkness. And yet, despite the fear surging through me, I knew it was close—closer than it had ever been, closer than I imagined it ever would be again.

Morning Light – Maples
There is an undeniable magic about the world when kissed by that early morning light. I guess you could say our journey that day, to that river, was in a way our perpetual morning—everything shone anew. The light filling our hearts and beaming forth from our eyes despite our weariness and fear made everything good again.

He stopped at the river. The water was shallow, but the rapids were strong. This was as far as he could take us. From here we had to go on foot. He made the sign of the cross and wished us the best. My mother and Oma as worn out as they were, knew we could not stop. The Russian army and Serbian guards hadn't broken us. The infested and toxic nature of our living conditions hadn't deterred us. Losing some of the people we held most dear hadn't weakened us. And this river, this final barrier between us and our freedom, would not stand in our way either.

Due to the fast current, my brother Bill had to carry me and Lisl across. Even today, I can still close my eyes and feel the icy cold of the water, I feel Bill shaking, a bit unsteady on the rocks, the trepidation of the moment, wondering if we truly would get to the shore. Next, he guided Mom and Oma across. He was the only one able to maneuver through the water while clutching his family close. When all was said and done, we made it, we were safe and we were still together.

There was a church to which we'd been instructed to go. Immediately we were ushered inside. My mother told us to change out of our wet clothes into the dry ones stored within our packs. That feeling of warmth against chilled, soaked skin was amazing—it felt safe. In fact, that little church was the safest place I'd been in for I don't know how long. We were to sleep by day and travel at night—the Austrian border now within a graspable distance. A washer woman arrived bearing a pail that was meant to serve as our toilet, along with some water to drink and bread and sausage for us to eat. Nothing tasted so good, or so real to me in some ways as that particular meal.

The sky was growing dark, this, I could make out through the high windows. Which meant that our sojourn at this warm and cozy little church was just about over. That's the thing about trying to escape—just when you get comfortable, just when you think you can finally drop your guard and maybe even close your eyes, you can't, not really. Not till you reach that place that represents the future for you and your family. For us, that place was Austria, and we were so close, so incredibly close.

A priest came to collect us, cramming my entire family into a tiny Volkswagen. I lay on the floor and so I couldn't really see much of what was transpiring. After what seemed like hours, he came to a stop. He directed us toward a high hill—over that hill, he explained, lay Austria. This was it; for weeks we'd traveled, and every day it was just a little closer. The life we'd run from, the torture we'd escaped… in a matter of a mere hike up the hillside—which, relatively speaking, seemed the easiest thing in the world—we'd never be subject to the horror again. We would be free. We would belong to ourselves and of course, to each other. The journey out of hell was nearly complete. And appropriately, in our assent, we'd be welcomed into heaven again.

The higher we got, the colder it became, until there was snow, and yet, we felt nothing, nothing but the exhilaration that was propelling us forward. Suddenly however, guards apparently on ski patrol spotted us and started in our direction. We all simultaneously broke out into a run while crying in lament. This couldn't be happening—not when we were this close, not when it was within reach. "Halt!" the men began screaming. And then they yelled: "You are in Austria now!" They weren't there to bring us back after all, they were there to help us move forward. I don't think even one of us remained standing. Everyone fell face first to the ground and kissed that snow... over and over and over again.

Terra Firma

Terra firma means dry land. Imagine you've come from the shaky seas, the raging rivers, whatever precarious form of traveling you'd undertaken and now you were there—on terra firma. And yet, while beyond grateful, you still had no idea what to expect or what lay ahead in your journey. It is good, but it is uncertain too.

CHAPTER 10

The Feeling of Freedom

We were taken to an Austrian refugee center in Gratz. With the influx of people from all over the neighboring regions, the Austrians had established these assembly centers to help keep things organized and most importantly, ease the refugees into this new freedom that had been stolen from them for so long.

They registered us, we were given the means to clean up; we were given beds and food. It was the first time in years things felt normal despite how unfamiliar the setting. But "normal" comes to have a whole new connotation when faced with the circumstances with which we'd dealt. Clean sheets, warm food, access to a school even—these were normal. Wonderfully, happily normal.

Mid November 1948, we were taken to an official refugee camp in the province of Karnten; it was called Feffernitz. The train ride there was quite literally like moving slow motion through the gates of heaven—it was a different world, one marked by beautiful stone houses, flower boxes everywhere, mountains and streams. I wouldn't budge from in front of the window. I wanted to take it all in, every single second. To be faced with so much beauty, after the darkness, I wanted to sing and laugh all in one breath, and I may have even wept tears of joy.

When we arrived, we were actually greeted by an Oomp-pa band—the boys in lederhosen, the girls in skirts. This couldn't be real, right? I had to be dreaming, I continuously told myself. The camp itself however, while certainly we were thankful, was a bit of a sobering experience, especially given the Valhalla like scenery which we encountered initially. The resettlement camp was basically a repurposed English barracks, fairly crude though we did have running water and electricity. There were no partitions separating one family from another. We changed behind blankets or in a dark corner and were given a mattress which Oma and my mother shared. And there was a small woodstove in the middle of our designated area that allowed us to keep warm.

My mother began working in the fields shortly after our arrival. She was to work at least two days a week in return for shelter and food, but my mother wanted more. She was stronger, and now that we were free and growing even stronger still, she worked six days a week. With the extra money she earned she purchased heavy cardboard, some wood and nails to make wall-like structures so that our family could have some privacy and better encapsulate the warmth from the stove.

We settled into life here. We'd line up twice a day to get our portion of food in a large, recycled bean can. And while in school there were ladies who brought us lunches. Not to mention, my mother eventually started working in a bakery as well as at the farm, which meant the occasional "surprise" food item on the night's menu. It was hard, often it was bitter cold even inside, and my brother Bill on occasion carried me to school because we had no shoes and the wet from the ground would freeze my feet—and yet, despite the circumstances, back then, at that moment in time, it was absolute bliss.

The Ant Trail
  "My child, behold the busy ant
  She knows what she's about;
  No unemployment in her midst
  Her purpose gives her clout."

School was huge for me. Up until then, I'd not just been isolated from education but from the everyday of what going to school represented. So many take it for granted, that it's there, that it's always going to be there. But when you're completely cut off from the academic and social environment of school it takes on a consequential new meaning. For me it did, for my brother, for Lisl…

We eventually came to hand sew mukluks from old canvas gotten off a neighboring chicken coop. As I said, school was monumental in my life and nothing was going to prevent me from going. The year of 1949 was a truly memorable one for a number of reasons, not the least of which was the basic fact that we were living our lives day to day, normal lives filled with laughter and light, school and even soccer. Yes, I joined the soccer team. I was a boy, living a boy's life. You don't understand how revelatory this was for me, for all of us. There was a point when we thought that nothing existed beyond death and mayhem. When you're immersed in the deepest pits of hell there is no door out, there is no tunnel guiding you toward light, toward a better day. There are only the flames licking your body, searing your skin, completely blinding you to the hope of any sort of good ever again. And then we escaped and hell slowly vanished, the flames smoldered until they were all but out and we were free, and yes, I was on the school soccer team.

I think back now to how unbelievably fast it all changed even though our escape may have seemed an eternity in the making. From dark to light, pain to promise, hell to heaven. No, we didn't have more than the barracks to live in with walls made of cardboard, but that was home in every sense of the word. My mother kept it clean and warm and even planted flowers outside. It was our present—and given the past we'd run from, there was no looking back.

Beyond my Mom, Oma, Bill, Lisl and I, there was also a young girl named Shirley who came into our lives during our years in the camp. She lived in the place next door to ours. It seemed she was with us though whenever she got the chance. Those who were looking after Shirley were older; they'd taken her in because she had no one following the war. Her mother was seemingly unreachable. And we were cramped, but we made room. Space gets redefined in places like that camp. The amount of space in light of the replenished joy and love in your heart becomes virtually limitless. We came to love Shirley like one of our own.

When the older couple's visa to America arrived, they had to leave Shirley behind. We gladly adopted her into our family. And we thought she'd be a part of us forever, so when her Hungarian mother at last showed up out of the blue, essentially, we were broken hearted. We did still see her at least monthly and for that we were thankful. Until eventually, she moved with her mom to Australia.

We also learned that my mother's sister Marianna was alive and well. She'd been taken to Russia three years before. Until that time, we'd known nothing of her fate. With the help of the Red Cross though, we located her and in 1949, she came home to us. The reunion was understandably a tearful one, and this was one of the first times since the war that I recall those tears being tears of pure happiness.

The thing about that time period, that specific year even, that most sticks out now decades later are the people. Our circumstances and life in the barracks aside, it was a moment of homecomings—historically so for us; it was also about meeting those who may have only been in our lives for a short time, but their presence was powerfully felt, and in some ways changed who we were.

Herr Sep for example became a prominent fixture in my life then. I called him my "Mountain Opa". I was wandering about looking for raspberry patches—Oma, Lisl and I sold berries to a wealthy baroness who had a processing business in which she made jams and jellies. She paid well for raspberries. Anyway, I was scouting new locations when I came upon an older man; he had a heavy beard but seemed inordinately gentle in his mannerisms. It was his land on which I apparently was looking for new berry patches. I apologized and he just smiled and invited us to lunch.

Oma, Lisl and I spent the afternoon visiting with Herr Sep. He told us about his family. His son was a doctor in a neighboring village. He then showed me his house and barn. I was awestruck; it was beautiful, the architecture so unique. Everything to include three small outbuildings appeared carved out of limestone. And happily, Herr Sep told me that I was welcomed to visit him whenever I had a chance. This was an offer that I most definitely took him up on—as over the course of the next couple of years, I was there practically every weekend. I hadn't realized how much I missed my grandfather—this is what Herr Sep became for me, this is the void he filled in my life. He taught me things, told me about the world, relayed stories of his life. Our bond was an important one for me. He'd even give me eggs, chicken, ham, you name it to bring home to mom and Oma. I never left empty-handed. His soul was gentle, his spirit beyond kind. That's why I say this time in our lives was as much about the people we encountered and subsequently let in, as it was about anything else.

The Twilight Years

This was of our sheltie. She is done in muted colors because her life is winding down, her spirit is tempering to a mellow gold. And yet always, that twinkle in her eye which foretold of mischievousness, passion, the will to persevere. I think now of Herr Sep very much along these lines. A man who'd mellowed and softened but never lost that essential spirit emblematic of who he was.

There are so many stories that I could tell here. So many memories and events—good and some bad too—that shaped our life while in the resettlement camp. For one thing, I was a boy scout—yes, I even got to be a boy scout, and because of my academic achievements I was rewarded with a chance to go on a two-week boy scout camp. It was absolutely amazing, up until I almost drowned, but fortunately my quick-thinking leader saved me. At one point I came to work for the rich baroness grooming her angora rabbits. My brother during this time was recognized as an outstanding high school student and as a result was able to attend a newly built school a few kilometers up the road. Bill and I became enthralled with the snow and building our own skiis. Saturday skiing became our ritual. I could go on of course, and that's the thing, that's the truly wonderful part about our life then, it's that I *can* go on. I do have such stories because my family and I made it through hell in order to create these stories and meet the special people we did.

We would ultimately leave Austria in 1951. The Red Cross had found my Uncle Peter and Great Uncle Wilhelm; they were in Windsor, Canada. They would become our sponsors. We were notified that within just a couple of months we'd be boarding an old, renovated cargo ship named Beaverbrae for Canada. That's it, our time in Austria, our life at the camp and the people with whom we'd forged important connections would be left behind. My parting from Herr Sep was particularly trying because I knew we'd never see one another again. We both cried so much our shirts were soaked from our tears.

Nightly Visitor

This is a story that I think extends to animals and humans alike. Our dog, Lily, always found her friends, among them, chipmunks and squirrels, near our compost pile. We were quite surprised when we came home one evening and saw Lily chase a raccoon up a tree. That wayward coon did not know that this fluffy puppy of ours was "all bark". But we certainly were glad that this wild wanderer decided to retreat. The following evening, and every evening thereafter, the masked bandit visited our compost pile. Our sheltie, in the meantime, toned down her bark and became timider with each nightly visit. The coon reciprocated. In fact, even our family was starting to look forward to seeing and talking to our newfound friend. Cautiously, Audrey and I watched as our children often threw him some supposedly stale food. As the summer passed, Lily stopped barking, and we fattened and befriended our nightly visitor. I guess it goes to show, you can be worlds apart as far as culture and background, experiences and attitudes, but if you take the time and nurture the relationship, you do come to see the value in the connections you make in this world.

Despite a bumpy journey fraught with much seasickness, we arrived in Halifax, Nova Scotia on May 7, 1951.

After a day or two, we boarded a train that would take us to Windsor and the family awaiting our arrival. As with any "homecoming" the tears flowed, hugs and smiles all around. Indeed, we were home, we'd made it to our version of heaven.

Epilogue

My life in Canada upon arriving in Windsor was I guess what you'd call typical. Of course, there were the ups and downs, highs and lows; as a family we cried, we laughed, fought, loved and ultimately cherished one another. This book though was meant to focus on a fairly specific, harrowing and life-altering moment in the trajectory of my 8+ decades here on earth. Though I do want to give you some insight into what did happen to us after we left the barracks and came to the place, we would call home for the rest of our lives…

Getting Situated & A Summer Away
For our first week in Windsor, we lived in a crowded (a.k.a. tiny) upstairs apartment, while my mother got to work trying to figure out how to pay off our sponsors. My mother's cousin had a farm—he offered Bill, a job; I would also come to work on that farm during the summer months. For the time being, there were a few weeks of school remaining. Even though I was thirteen at the time, I was actually placed in a Grade 1 class as I did not speak the language. Surprisingly, I enjoyed myself. The little kids got a kick out of my attempts at English pronunciation. And I enjoyed interacting with them. I worked hard though to improve; the teacher was extra supportive and within a few weeks, I was ready for Grade 4 material.

Then it was time for summer and a job working on a tobacco farm. Both Bill and I were given a room and board with my mother's cousin and consequently worked for ten and eight dollars a day respectively. I was sad to leave the city of Windsor for the season; after all that had happened, all of the relocations, I'd started to feel welcomed somewhere, truly so. I was making friends and learning English. I can't quite describe it, but something inside of me told me that this is where I was supposed to be. There was this undeniable connection with the city and its people. However, I would not disobey my mother and I knew we needed the money. So come June, Bill and I left to become farmhands.

Canadian Sunrise
Canada and all that it promised certainly was a wonder to my family and me. It was wide and expansive in so many ways, and despite any hardships we faced in those early days, this amazing country and its scenic landscapes drew from our hearts that same feeling of expansiveness. I think more so than anything, as a young boy having come to this country from what I'd experienced and the life I'd lived before, I reveled in the sheer freedom of the moments I had—each one of them.

Living with my brother under these circumstances was trying, to say the least. Perhaps to impress our hosts, he seemed to want to dictate my every move, from how I folded my clothes to how our shared bed was made. Not the most pleasant start to our summer with him playing father, but I appreciated his love and concern.

However, for the most part that summer proved fairly routine. I must say though that as it was my job to unload the tobacco boats for the ladies who'd then tie them together and fill the racks for the kiln, I was indoctrinated into what some might call the coarser side of life on the tobacco farm. These women were certainly different from my mother and Oma. They spoke quite openly about affairs and their sexual exploits. I can only imagine that they were trying to corrupt a naïve fourteen-year-old boy; accordingly, I'd blush and stammer until I, eventually, learned to grow a thicker skin.

I remember this one incident… Some dry tobacco leaves had fallen on the furnace, the kiln was almost instantly ablaze. The horses tied up were understandably in a panic. I grabbed one of the lady's jackets and covered the head of a horse that was tied up nearby. Using my knife, I cut him loose and led him away. The local paper called me a hero. One of the women who particularly enjoyed tormenting me even heralded my amazing efforts. I don't know about all that, but I certainly remember the adrenaline rushing through me as I worked to save that terrified creature.

Something Unexpected
Come September, life would again change. My brother Bill would take a job with General Motors, and as for me, after meeting with the principal of the school and demonstrating to him how far my English had improved, he recommended that I go to Grade seven. I was ecstatic. I skipped all the way home only to encounter a strange man standing next to my mother. Mom and Oma were anxiously awaiting my return, eager to introduce me to the widower who would become my stepfather.

Mike seemed like a decent enough guy. He had three grown children and his wife had recently passed. Despite any hesitations I may have had, my mom was 37, she'd been through hell and back, she'd nearly died more than once in her efforts to safeguard her family. She deserved some piece of happiness, something that she could grasp onto with both hands and call a normal life. And in our case, normal was everything.

The Meeting

Love is important; what's more, being able to share your highs and lows, your happy days and the sad with someone special can mean the difference between a life worth living and one in which you merely go through the motions. I know for me this is the case. And I know for my mother, deep down, she wanted that partner she'd once had in my father but so tragically lost. She wanted to feel anchored somehow, that intrinsic sense of belonging. And so, she turned to Mike...

I myself don't think I've ever taken for granted the normalcy of a happy marriage, or of being a father, of watching my kids grow up, of ultimately becoming a teacher. I think more so than most I have been granted that once-in-a-lifetime ability to actually see and appreciate the so-called "normal" for what it is—absolute heaven. And at that time, in that moment, I remember hoping as I stood there, albeit somewhat awkwardly, in front of this stranger named Mike, that my mother's absolute heaven was now. That she'd be loved and cared for. That she'd have a partner again on whom she could lean whenever she felt tired or weary. She deserved it… If only.

Life with Mike

We moved to Blenheim in 1952. My mother and Mike had had a civil union drawn up and they'd found a 100-acre farm to share crop. Mike's youngest son Joe still lived with him and so he too became a part of my newly blended family. Initially farm life, especially with the friendship of my stepbrother, was fine.

There were ducks, geese, chickens and horses. I enjoyed helping Joe with them, but then as with many a situation when people become comfortable, when they start to shed the veneer of the front that they tend to put on sometimes when things are new and they are trying to portray a better, not necessarily "real" side, this is when things devolve and begin to get bad.

Mike, at least the Mike who first won over my mother, was not the Mike I came to live with on that farm. I first started to see the façade crumble in how he treated his own son. And then it was me too. It was never enough—whatever we did, however hard we tried, he was dissatisfied with our efforts. For instance, I remember the cold. The house was freezing, and our only source of heat was a woodstove. Mike, Mom and Oma slept around it. Joe and I huddled under quilts and whatever blankets we had in our respective rooms. One morning Mike raced upstairs bellowing: 'Who let the woodstove run out?' We would subsequently not be served breakfast until there was a fully stacked pile. He was a man who seemingly refused to see beyond what you did wrong—you were accordingly harassed because of mistakes or sometimes, especially in the case of Joe, for just existing in his presence.

Abandoned Homestead
    Spent Dreams
    High and lofty empty room
    How solitary they stand;
    Held together with rusty nails
    And spent dreams.

His temperament toward my mother and Oma wasn't much better, although he and my mom did have farming in common. I could tell he enjoyed talking to her about it, particularly because she was so knowledgeable about crops and planting. In fact, my mother became the mastermind of that farm, selling a bumper crop of potatoes one year (when the rest of the region was having a difficult time of it) for $10,000. About that, Mike was at least happy.

A Farm of Our Own

The following year, my mother had put away enough to purchase our own farm: hundred acres in West Lorne. I loved that place, probably because I associate it with one of the first times I got to draw and paint in earnest. Not just with sticks and mud this time but actual paper and watercolors. Mr. Quigley, I will always remember him as one of my first mentors. He was my teacher and he saw in me what I knew was there but had been reluctant to give actual voice to, probably because of all that I had endured. Art for me had been a means of survival. Yes, I'd also used my art to try and lighten the mood and the moment for those imprisoned with me, but it was inherently private at its heart. It was in some senses my way of dreaming beyond the confines of the horrific real. It was the embodiment of my hope—the hope we all harbored, though we didn't dare speak of it. My art spoke for me.

Daisy

Art can be found in the simplest object—in something you might not even notice otherwise. This flower, for instance, potentially trod upon if not looked for… And yet to the ladybug exploring its valleys and peaks, it is everything in that moment. This is what art represents for me—especially then, when first entering this world of objects and their consequent impressions: the scene or object I was seeing and the way in which it came to be everything, at least in that moment.

And here, for perhaps the very first time, someone else, a teacher, was looking at my work; he was evaluating it and he ultimately saw the potential in it. In fact, Mr. Quigley had one of my paintings framed and entered it into the West Elgin District Fair. I won first place. With the glorious honor came twenty dollars, plus a woman bought the painting for twenty-five. I had money now to purchase that which was my destiny: my own paints.

It was painting and also school itself, the running track and becoming involved in extracurricular activities, that kept me busy and happy. The farm also took its share of work and time, and that was okay; it at least gave me something to do while at home, something besides dealing with the wrath of Mike or bearing witness to the crumbling façade that once upon a time was my mother's happiness. Mike's growing anger touched all our lives.

There was this one incident when we were stacking bundles of wheat. One bundle that I'd thrown to the top came tumbling down. Mike kicked me and then aimed his pitchfork at me. My stepbrother Joe and Bill thankfully intervened. Joe practically growled at his father: 'If you ever touch him again, I will kill you!' I'd never seen him so forceful or quite so incensed. I looked at Joe very differently after that. And Mike never did lay a finger on me again.

When not bundling wheat or capturing the images around the farm with my paints, I could generally be found in the company of my horses, Dick and Tom, and my dog, Sport. I adored those animals. I still adore animals. There's something so pure about an animal's response to the world around them. Look into their eyes, watch their expressions and there's inevitably this innate goodness that isn't out to deceive or manipulate—they are exactly who they show themselves to be. There aren't too many humans about whom you can say that.

Broken Silence
I painted these horses, the black and white together, because I see in their symbolic stance, that which should be endemic to all human beings. Not just in terms of different races, cultures and societies, but in terms of how hearts need to bind together, understand one another. Perhaps one of the greatest tragedies of the world we live in now is the presence of these internal barriers with which we shield our hearts. We fail to extend to others kindness and decency because we won't allow our hearts to be that vulnerable or open. Whereas animals, like these horses, possess a pureness that humans can't seem to duplicate regardless of how hard we try.

Mike, however, did not see their goodness or their pureness. One of the more distressing moments I witnessed was when our wagon was stuck in the mud loaded down heavily with tree branches and trunks. Dick and Tom could not pull it out. Mike thought the solution was therefore to whip them until by some miracle the power of pain would imbue them with the strength to dislodge the wagon wheels. Of course, that didn't happen. All that happened was that my beloved ponies were covered in welts and sores. Mike stormed off when his brutal tactics failed. Oma, Mom and I proceeded to rub a mixture of Schnapps and lard on the poor horses' welts. Mike refused to deal with those animals from that point on, for which I was thankful. But again, it was easy to see how the longer our tenure on that farm, the longer the marriage persisted, the meaner and more abusive toward people and animals alike, this man became.

We also had cows. When one of them gave birth, my mother let me keep the bull; I proceeded to name him Bengel, namesake to the sheep that Bill and I lost in Molidorf. I played with Bengel every single day. I fed him by hand, rubbed his head and stomach. I even managed to teach him commands—no lie. He comprehended 'Wait,' 'Be nice' when he started acting up, as well as being responsive to his name. I was quite proud of this accomplishment. Mostly, I adored just spending time with my Bengel. As he grew—and boy did he grow—he became something of a prized stud. Neighbors paid good money to mate their cows with Bengel.

This all changed however when he turned three. Mike was bringing the cows in. Bengel hesitated. Mike, grabbing a fencepost club, hit the bull squarely between the eyes, knocking him out cold. Bengel regained consciousness, but it was as if Mike's anger, his violence, had beaten the good and the sensible out of that animal. The bull thus became volatile. Unless you approached him club in hand, he was threatening. It was a completely different creature—one I did not know. In fact, one afternoon, out of the corner of my eye, I spotted him gearing up to charge me; I called out his name, I screamed 'wait' and 'be nice,' nothing. Mike may not have killed him, but looking into his eyes, I could see that my Bengel was dead.

I made it to the fence and started frantically climbing over it but not before he managed to hit me squarely on my lower back. I flew over the fence and landed in a manure pile. Mike, witnessing what'd transpired, had a good laugh. I however had a broken tailbone. To this day, I still experience pain as a result of Mike's transmogrification of a once noble animal.

My Mother: An Agricultural Phenom
I can't say enough about my mother's heart, her spirit, her generosity, and certainly, there was also her intelligence—especially when it came to agriculture. She'd run the estate in Molidorf; she understood planting cycles; she knew what crops were needed in order to not only grow but do so bountifully. She had the ultimate green thumb you might say. And as such, Heinz of Ontario paid us well for growing eighteen acres of

tomatoes for them. Mike, in one of his softer moments, called my mother the "sergeant". She gave orders and we followed; amazingly even Mike and I managed to work side by side under my mother's directives.

Farmscape – Turbulent Sky
A farmer's life is precarious indeed. You are at the mercy of Mother Nature and her fickle weather patterns. I know that living on the farm as a boy, working with Mike and my mom, there were days we didn't know what to expect. But that was the thing about my mom… Perhaps because she was a woman, she was exceedingly in tune with the whims of mighty Mother Nature; she had this uncanny ability to see the bigger picture that lay ahead. She was truly something special.

One year, an early frost nearly wiped out the tomato crops in the region, except ours of course because of my mother's skill and foresight. That year, with only about five farms still possessing a tomato crop, my mother made enough to pay off the farm.

Sometimes however, I think my mother tried to take on a bit too much. There was this one time she was out pulling weeds in the soybean field. She was attempting to scale a rusty old fence. Her foot must've gotten hooked because she fell backward, in the process actually snapping her back. She lay immobile and in agonizing pain. No one was around or within ear shot.

No one that is except for Sport. She called to the dog and bade him to 'go and fetch Peter!' Yes, my Sport was every bit the Lassie. He did come and get me; I found my mother and ultimately brought the paramedics to her.

She remained in the hospital for three months. She had to relearn how to walk upon getting out. Given everything she'd experienced in a lifetime, walking again was a challenge she gladly undertook.

The End of an Era
Life on that farm had its ups and downs, but I always knew Joe would be there for me, he had my back as they say. Until he wasn't there anymore. Until he simply couldn't take it anymore. Being Mike's step-son was difficult. It came with humiliation, sometimes pain, anger, sadness—the gamut of negative emotions. Being Mike's son was all of this but worse. Joe felt the brunt of his father's general animosity toward the human spirit. He was beaten, belittled and finally, he broke. It's a funny thing though, when you're broken, you realize in some ways there's nothing left to lose.

At the camp, we were all in the process of being broken, over and over. Toward the end, there was that part of us that felt as though there was nothing left to lose. Our humanity had been taken, our bodies starved and debilitated, and so over and over people would try to escape despite the terrifying consequences of being caught. This was Joe's escape. Except that he was nineteen and he was free and he had the means of moving away from the tyrant who would otherwise seek to destroy him a little more each day. Not to mention, he was repulsed by the thought of growing up and becoming a man like his father.

I was devastated to be losing yet another brother. We wept upon our parting. My mother assured him that we would always remember him and always love him. Joe made good on his vow not to be like his dad. He eventually would open a construction company, marry and have two beautiful girls. He and his wife Gwen would later build and run the Crown Motor Motel until his wife's death, after which Joe retired. He and my brother Bill are still the best of friends and see each other often. And I am so glad that he came into my life when he did. As I've said, the best parts of life and memories are the good people we are fortunate enough to meet and keep with us in our hearts and minds.

Time to Reflect

Throughout my life, there have been moments and times when I needed to step away and just reflect. I had to think about the experiences I endured—what thoughts they provoked in me, what emotions they conjured. And so, in many of my paintings, there is this deeply ingrained spirit of reflection present, both in terms of the subject and also in terms of what the viewer sees, where his/her eyes go, what spaces within the frame of the work they focus in on and consequently what thoughts this then evokes in them.

Shortly after Joe moved out, my mother and Mike's marriage would come to an end. With my mother's back preventing her from being the work horse Mike once took such great pride in, the tensions grew. Mike resented her not helping on the farm and without Joe things were woefully shorthanded. They started discussing a separation—it was inevitable. A marriage simply cannot be sustained based upon a working relationship and lacking any softness or love. Mike would deride my mother, insisting that as her back hindered her from "earning her keep" no one would want her after that. He didn't know my mother at all…

Back to Windsor and Beyond

As soon as I finished grade 12, my mother, Oma and I moved back to Windsor. I was ecstatic to be starting my last year of high school and preparing for college—I was ecstatic to be away from Mike. However, this period was met with sadness as well. Oma grew weaker; she had to be hospitalized. I went and visited her whenever I could. I will never ever forget those last words she uttered to me after telling me how much she loved me, and how wonderful a life she knew I would lead, she said: 'I must leave you now.' She died on my birthday. Her story ended on that day; her spirit never will.

The following year I was off to Teachers College. I stayed with Miss Monroe who let out rooms in her home to generate needed income. Twenty-three dollars a week and she kept our rooms tidy and our bellies full.

My time in college was filled with some great friendships, my share of fun, some youthful hijinks, and of course studying. As always, I was diligent about my work. I wanted to teach, to try and impact the lives of young people as mine had been impacted by so many of my teachers along the way. I wanted to instill in them a sense of citizenship and responsibility for one's fellow human beings. And it's important to note that my teachers, such who had taught me the importance of these things, hadn't been strictly teachers in the professional sense. It was also my mother, Oma, my grandfather, Herr Sep even. People who took the time to show me whether directly or by example what it was to be a good person at heart and to always try and live according to your best intentions.

I took those lessons to my first job at King George Elementary School. There I taught art to grades 4 through 8; I was in heaven. I got them drawing and painting from the heart—getting messy on occasion, but whoever said creativity isn't messy sometimes. Inspired by the slides of professional artists and my own artwork, they willingly displayed their work at various local art shows. It was truly gratifying, and I could not have asked for a better start to my teaching career.

Panoramic with Red-Tailed Hawk
I liken my college years and experiences in some ways to this particular composition. There was so much to do, see, and take in. So many people with whom to interact and from whom to gain new insights and knowledge. Education is something I've always prized, quite possibly because I was deprived of it during those horrific early years. Like this hawk soaring, the sky is the limit when you set out on your quest to learn and consequently grow.

Love Comes Softly

1960 would mark one of the most important years in my life: it was the year I met my wife, Audrey. New Year's Eve, some friends and I were part of a group, the Teutonia Club, that met on occasion for dances. She was there. She was sitting all by herself, seemingly shy and quiet. She was beautiful; I was immediately drawn to her quiet beauty and what I imagined was a generous soul. I took a chance—she agreed to dance with me and we practically spent the remainder of the evening dancing, laughing and talking. In the course of our twirling about the dance floor, we even discovered that my mother knew her parents as they attended the same church. Even though it was a first dance followed by a second and sometime later that night, a tenth, I somehow knew I would never let her leave my arms.

We were married in May of 1962. Shortly after we were wed, I was transferred to F.W. Begley Public School, not exactly the same socio-economic makeup as that of King George. Kids would fall asleep in class.

Some would come in with bruises. They'd come in crying about their parents' constant drunkenness. There was no end to what these kids had faced in their young lives. One of my eighth-grade students had even been raped by four teenagers. I was devastated. I tried to talk to her, to convey some of the horrors that I'd faced, not by way of comparison, but in order to try and show her that the human spirit is resilient beyond what we might think. She was young, she had an entire life ahead and it was her responsibility to live it the best way she could—not let her attackers take that from her. I think she might've gotten the message. Four years later I attended her graduation. She introduced me to a young man who I could tell was someone special.

During this time, I also became a father—one of the most important roles in my life. Our daughter Eileen was born in 1963 and Mark a year later in 1964. The joy added to mine and Audrey's lives was immeasurable. This was a heaven I never knew existed.

Angelic Sleep
How angelic a baby is in their sleep and how we also cherish those quiet moments…

The Artist

I at last attained an Art Specialist Degree and an Honor B.A, neither of which would have been possible without my wife, and not simply in her role as keeper of the hearth, but additionally as my editor and devoted typist. I took on a new teaching position while also diligently working on my own art. Throughout the years I have had my own art in a variety of juried exhibitions to include showings at the University of Windsor in 1970 and 1982, St. Clair College in 1972, the Windsor Southwest Exhibition of 1971, 1972, 1975, and 1978 at the Art Gallery of Windsor. I won the prestigious 'Mae Hull Drawing Award'; the LaCloche Art Show of Northern Ontario from 1986 to present. Manitowaning Art Show in 1984, Leamington Art Gallery in 1985, St. Matthews Gallery 1986, Windsor Board of Education 1989, Art Gallery of Windsor Rental Gallery 1976-1986, Perivale Gallery for several years, Art After All 2003, Centennial Museum 2009, 2012, 2013, 2014, 2014, 2015, Nemi Public Library 2013, 2015, Turners' Gallery of Little Current 2005 to present. There are several hundred pieces of my art in circulation, with many of them in private collections in Canada, Unites States and Europe.

And I have been honored and humbled by all of this, but it's been the teaching that has meant the most to me. I paint and draw because I was born to do so. It's how I express when I am happy, or frightened or angry, or sad, what have you. Art is also my escape. It was Thomas Merton who said: "Art enables us to find ourselves and lose ourselves at the same time." That is true on so many levels. But with teaching, there is a solidity and wholeness to my purpose that is undeniable. It wasn't lecturing on the mechanics of art or even art history—it was about inspiring, helping kids to tap into whatever emotional resources they had inside and convey this in an artistic format. And at the same time, reinforcing the importance of being good citourns not just of their town or of Canada, but of the world, first and foremost.

My life since the camp and all that we saw and personally suffered, has been a heavenly journey—there is no other way I can think to describe it. Some might say given the hand I was dealt early in life, my outlook is way too optimistic, too charitable even. But it was because of my experiences that I understand what good is, what wonderful is, and certainly what heaven is.

Life's Wonderment

In many ways, this painting says it all. How we see the world, how we understand the journey we are on is highly subjective. Someone can look at a simple flower and see a marvelous cosmos. Another can view that same flower and see only its flaws. Life is a series of moments during which we are constantly discovering, constantly experiencing. For the most part, I am happy to say I have chosen to see the wonder and beauty in those moments and experiences. I am an artist after all.

Heaven is catching the eye of a quiet and shy woman at a dance and working up the courage to ask her to accompany you on the floor. Heaven is having students who listen to what you say and work hard to put it into practice and then thank you for inspiring them. Heaven is watching two tiny human beings that you helped create see the world for the first time. Heaven is a day spent at your lake house watching your grandchildren laugh and play. Heaven is your colleagues and friends shouting surprise at your retirement party. Heaven is having a mother for whom you are beyond grateful be with you until the age of 96. Heaven is when people look at your art and feel that they know what was in your heart when you painted it. Heaven is all of these things and so much more, because when it comes right down to it—heaven is living. If my life journey has taught me anything, it taught me that.